Top Kids 3

Judy Baldwin • Lisa Kingsley

Seed Learning

Top Kids 3 Student Book

Judy Baldwin / Lisa Kingsley

Acquisitions Editor: Casey Malarcher

Content Editor: Kelly Daniels

Copy Editor: Samantha Town

Design: AC Estudio Editorial SL

Illustrators: Ángeles Peinador, Javier Monsalvett, Jocar, Miguel Calero

Typeset: Integra Software Services Pvt. Ltd.

The authors would like to acknowledge Joy Yongo for contributing material to this book.

http://www.seed-learning.com

ISBN: 978-1-944879-66-2

10 9 8 7 6 5 4 3 2
21 20 19 18

TABLE OF CONTENTS

In the Neighborhood

Words

A. Track 2 Listen and point. **B.** Track 3 Listen and say.

C. Point and say.

1.  park
2.  library
3.  bakery
4.  store
5.  school
6.  house

D. Remember. Use your book. Point and say.

Patterns

A. Track 4 Listen and say.

B. Read the sentences. Write the words.

1

Where's she ________________ ?

She's ________________ to the bakery.

2

Where's he ________________ ?

He's ________________ to the library.

3

________________ he going?

________________ going home.

4

________________ she going?

________________ going to the store.

C. Practice with a partner. Use your books.

Words

A. Track 5 Listen and point. **B.** Track 6 Listen and say. **C.** Point and say.

1 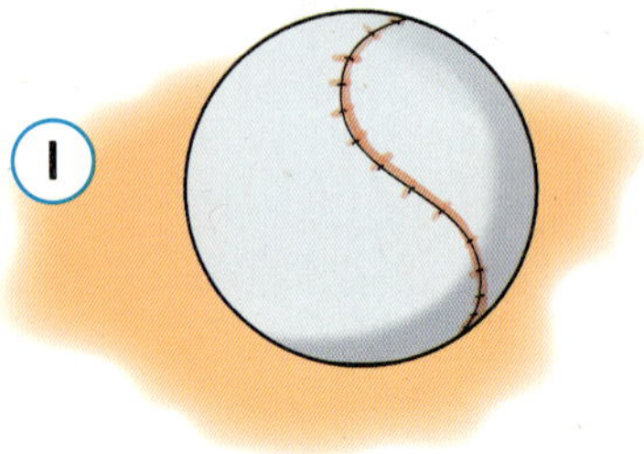

baseball

2 

storybook

3 

apple pie

4 

egg

5 

workbook

6 

key

D. Look and write.

1 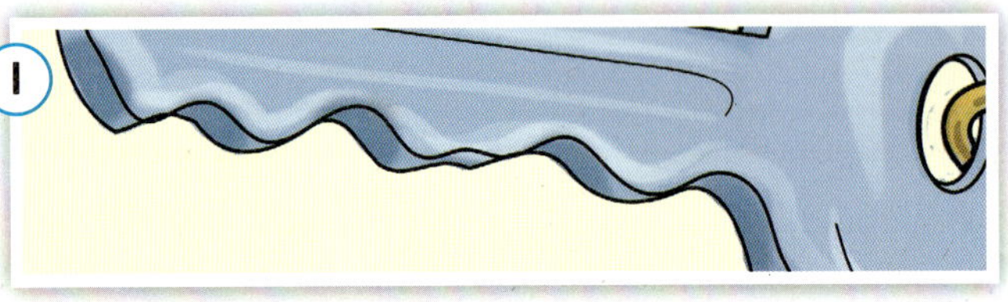

It's a ______________________________ .

2 

It's an ______________________________ .

3 

It's a ______________________________ .

4 

It's a ______________________________ .

E. Remember. Practice with a partner.

Patterns

A. Track 7 Listen and say.

B. Read the sentences. Write the words.

1. She ________ an apple pie.

2. He ________ a storybook.

3. ________ has a key.

4. ________ has eggs.

C. Talk about your classmates' things.

D. Track 8 Sing the song. Go to page 76.

Conversation

A. Track 9 Listen and point.

B. Track 10 Listen and say.

C. Track 11 Listen. Practice with the new words.

So do I. beautiful

D. Role-play the dialogue.

E. **Value** Write a check (✓) or an (✗).

1

2

3

Sounds

A. Track 12 Listen and say.

Long a

cake

paint

gray

B. Track 13 Listen. Write a check (✓) if the word has a *long a* sound.

1 

2 

3 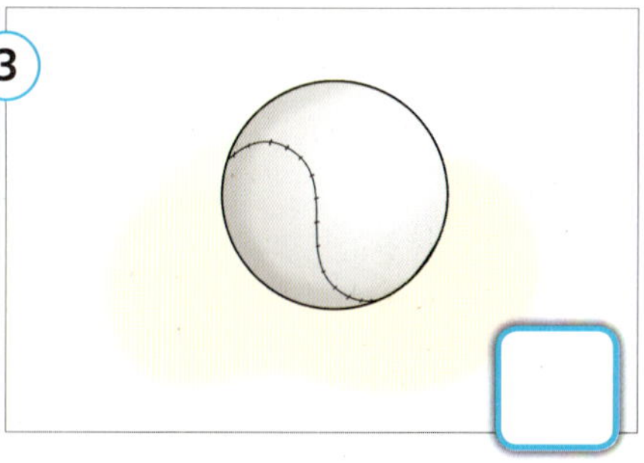

4 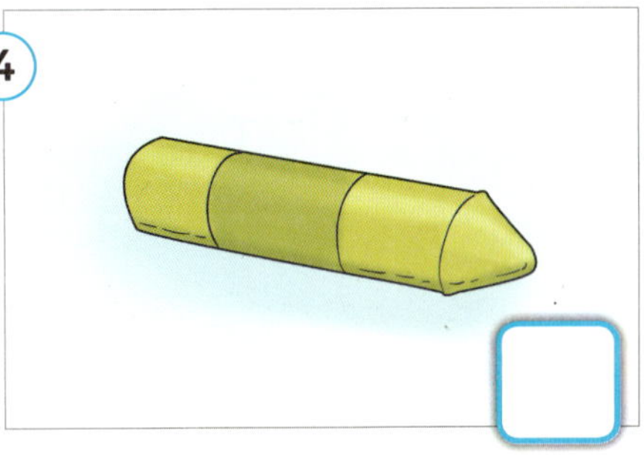

5 

6 

C. Track 14 Listen and match.

1 2 3 4 5

main game face tail day

D. Read the words.

a – e	ai	ay
same	gain	play
take	wait	say

Expansion 1

A. Look, read and circle.

1. He's going to the bakery. / store.

2. She's going to school. / the park.

3. He's going to the bakery. / library.

4. She's going home. / to school.

B. Look, read and write.

1. She has a ____________.
2. He has an ____________.
3. She has a ____________.
4. He has a ____________.

C. What about you? Read, check (✓) and write.

1. I like
   - ☐ my school.
   - ☐ the park.
   - ☐ the library.

2. I have
   - ☐ a storybook.
   - ☐ a workbook.
   - ☐ a baseball.

3. I live in ______________. It's a ☐ friendly ☐ beautiful place.

D. Project. Draw your home. Talk about your neighborhood.

Unit 2

Pets

Words

A. Track 15 Listen and point.

B. Track 16 Listen and say.

C. Point and say.

1.  kitten
2.  puppy
3.  goldfish
4.  hamster
5.  turtle
6.  parrot

D. Remember. Talk about yourselves.

Patterns

A. Track 17 Listen and say.

B. Read the sentences. Write the words.

1

He ________ ________ a parrot.

2

She ________ ________ a turtle.

3

She ________ ________ a hamster.

4

He ________ ________ a kitten.

C. Practice with a partner. Talk about your classmates.

Words

A. Track 18 Listen and point. **B.** Track 19 Listen and say. **C.** Point and say.

1 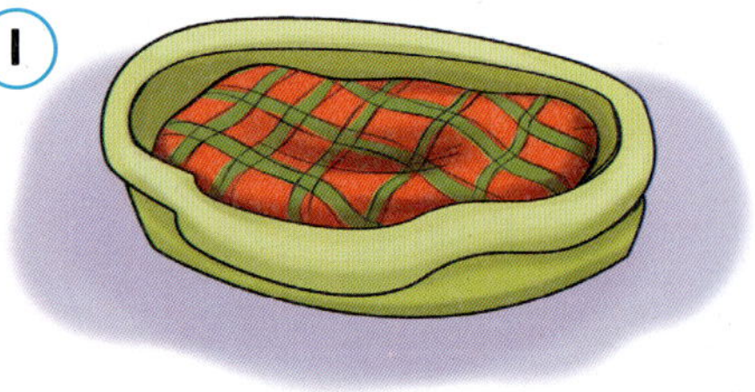

dog bed

2 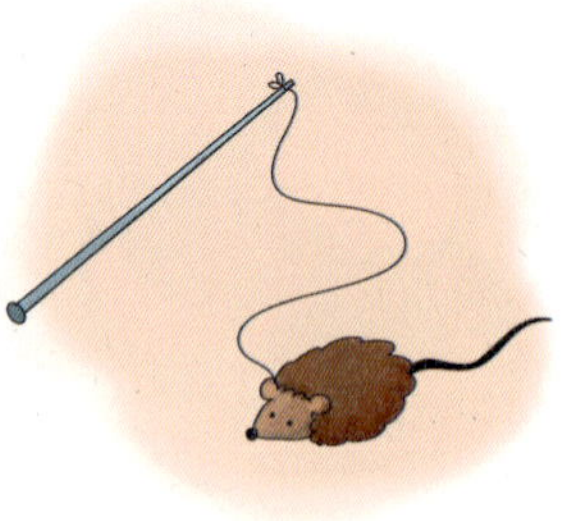

cat toy

3 

goldfish bowl

4 

dog house

5 

pet food

6 

hamster cage

D. Look, read and write.

1. He has a ______________ .
2. She has a ______________ .
3. He has a ______________ .
4. It has a ______________ .

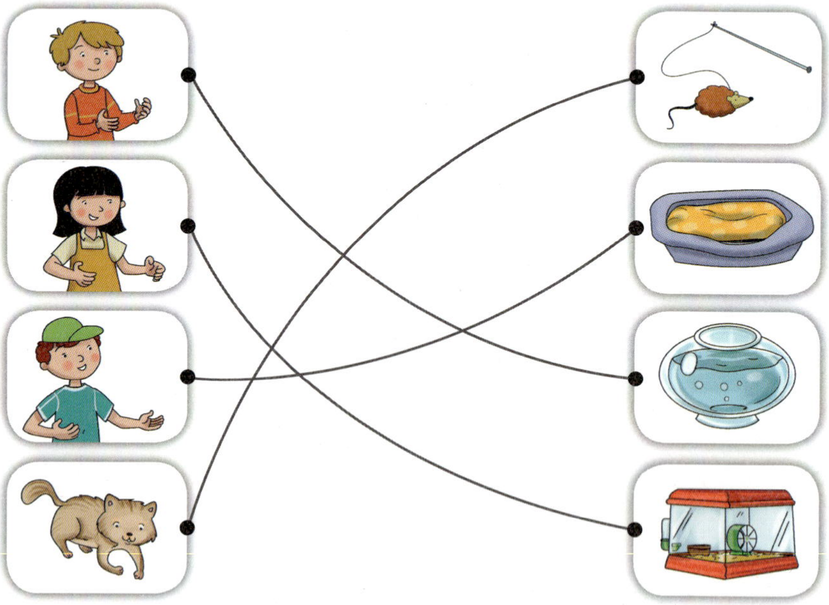

E. Remember. Draw and guess.

Patterns

A. Track 20 Listen and say.

B. Read the sentences. Write the words.

1. What ______ he ______?

He ______ a goldfish bowl.

2. What ______ she ______?

She ______ a cat toy.

3. What ______ she ______?

She ______ pet food.

4. What ______ he ______?

He ______ a dog house.

C. Practice with a partner. Use your books.

D. Track 21 Sing the song. Go to page 76.

Conversation

A. Track 22 Listen and point.

B. Track 23 Listen and say.

C. Track 24 Listen. Then practice with the new words.

big   You're welcome

D. Role-play the dialogue.

E. **Value** Write a check (✓) or an (✗).

1 

2 

3 

Sounds

A. Track 25 Listen and say.

Long a

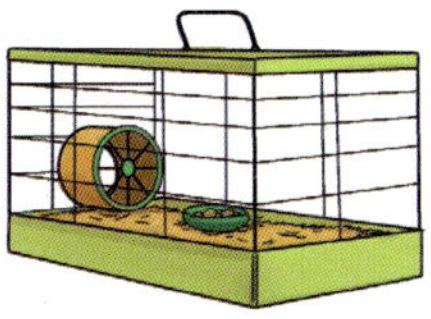
cage

play

rain

Short a

bag

cat

pan

B. Track 26 Listen and circle.

1 
long a   short a

2 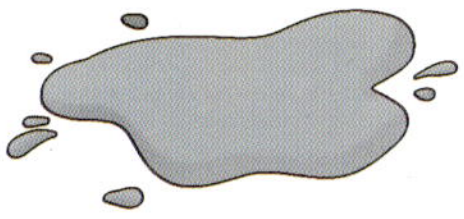
long a   short a

3 
long a   short a

4 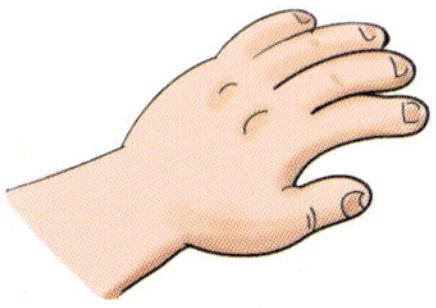
long a   short a

5 
long a   short a

6 
long a   short a

C. Track 27 Listen and check (✓).

1. ☐ cap
   ☐ cape
2. ☐ man
   ☐ main
3. ☐ pad
   ☐ paid
4. ☐ rat
   ☐ rate

D. Read the words.

1.	2.	3.	4.
fade	fad	bait	bat
laid	lad	hate	hat
made	mad	mate	mat

Reading 1

Herby Gets a Pet

A. Track 28 Listen and follow along.

Herby has toys.
He has friends.
But Herby doesn't have a pet.
Herby is sad.

What is Herby doing?
He's looking for a pet.
Puppies and kittens are too big.
Parrots are too scary.

Look! Herby has a pet!
It's an ant.
Her name is Ann.
Herby is happy.
Ann is happy, too.

D. Read and write *Yes* or *No*.

______ **1.** Herby doesn't have friends.

______ **2.** Herby has a pet ant.

B. Track 29 Listen, read and say.

C. Read with a partner.

Herby is very busy.
Herby gives Ann food.
He gives Ann water.
He gives Ann a bed and a toy.

Herby and Ann are together every day.
They play together.
They sing together.
Pets are fun.

Herby loves Ann.
Ann loves Herby, too.

New Words: • pet • look for • give • together • love

______ **3.** Herby gives Ann a cage.

______ **4.** Herby and Ann sing and play together.

Unit 3

After School

Words

A. Track 30 Listen and point. **B.** Track 31 Listen and say.

C. Point and say.

1. Monday 5 January
2. Tuesday 6 January
3. Wednesday 7 January
4. Thursday 8 January
5. Friday 9 January
6. Saturday 10 January
7. Sunday 11 January

D. Remember. Talk about yourselves.

Patterns

A. Track 32 Listen and say.

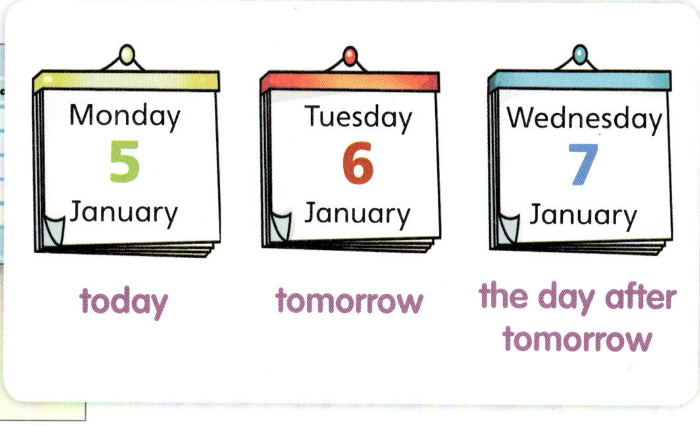

B. Read the sentences. Write the words.

1

______ day ______ tomorrow?

______ Saturday.

2

______ day ______ the day after tomorrow? ______ Thursday.

3

______ day ______ today?

______ Tuesday.

4

______ day ______ tomorrow?

______ Sunday.

C. Practice with a partner.

Words

A. Track 33 Listen and point. **B.** Track 34 Listen and say. **C.** Point and say.

1

English class

2

math class

3

computer class

4

music class

5

kung fu class

6

ballet class

D. Look and write.

1

He's going to ________ ________.

2

She's going to ________ ________.

3

She's going to ________ ________.

4

He's going to ________ ________.

E. Remember. Talk about yourselves.

Patterns

A. Track 35 Listen and say.

B. Read the sentences. Write the words.

1

They _______ ballet class _______ Tuesday.

2

She _______ computer class _______ Monday.

3

You _______ kung fu class _______ Thursday.

4

We _______ math class _______ Wednesday.

C. Practice with a partner. Talk about yourselves.

D. Track 36 Sing the song. Go to page 77.

Conversation

A. Track 37 Listen and point.

B. Track 38 Listen and say.

C. Track 39 Listen. Then practice with the new words.

come to my house | ballet

D. Role-play the dialogue.

E. **Value** Write a check (✓) or an (✗).

1

2

3

Sounds

A. Track 40 Listen and say.

Long e

bee

jeep

eat

leaf

B. Track 41 Listen. Circle the words with a *long e* sound.

1 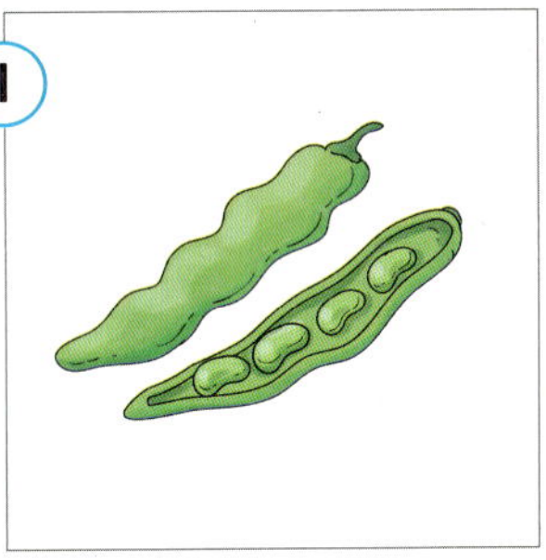

2 

3 

4 

5 

6 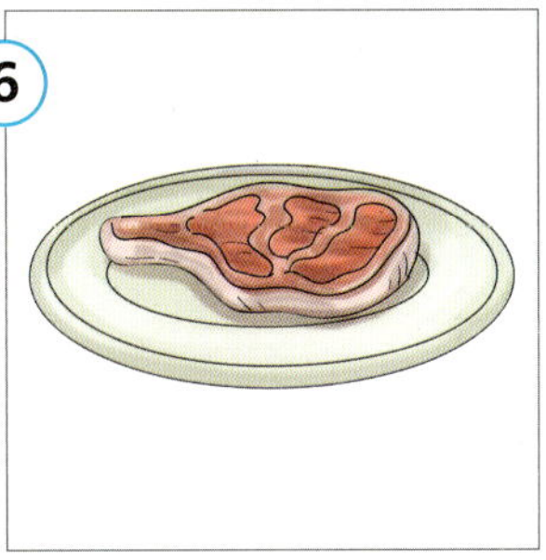

7 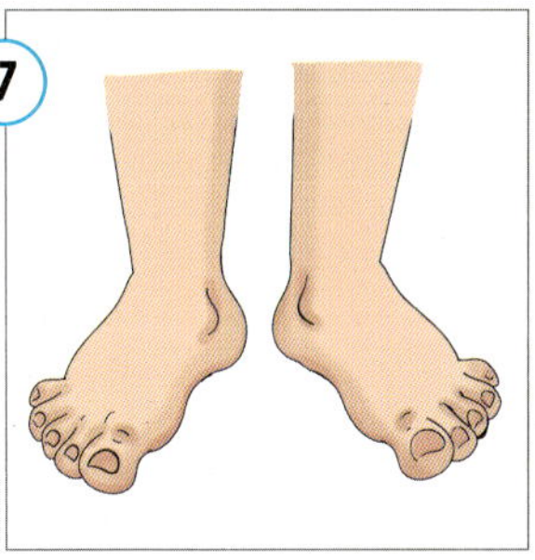

8 

C. Track 42 Listen and match.

1.
b t
ea
m d

2.
r k
ee
w d

3.
h p
ea
l d

4.
s n
ee
t d

D. Read the words.

1. need
seed
weed

2. beak
leak
weak

3. bean
lean
mean

4. feel
heel
peel

Expansion 2

A. Read and write.

1. Today is Friday. What day is tomorrow?

   ________________________________ .

2. Today is Sunday. What day is the day after tomorrow?

   ________________________________ .

3. Tomorrow is Thursday. What day is today?

   ________________________________ .

4. The day after tomorrow is Monday. What day is today?

   ________________________________ .

B. Look. Write an X on the one that doesn't belong. Then write.

1 

She has ____________ ____________
on Saturday.

2 

He has ____________ ____________
on Friday.

3 

She has ____________ ____________
on Tuesday.

4 

He has ____________ ____________
on Wednesday.

C. What about you? Read and write.

1. Today is ______________ .

   Tomorrow is ______________ .

   My favorite day is ______________ .

2. I like ☐ English class.

   ☐ math class.

   ☐ music class.

3. I have to practice ______________ .

D. Project. Complete the calendar. Talk about it.

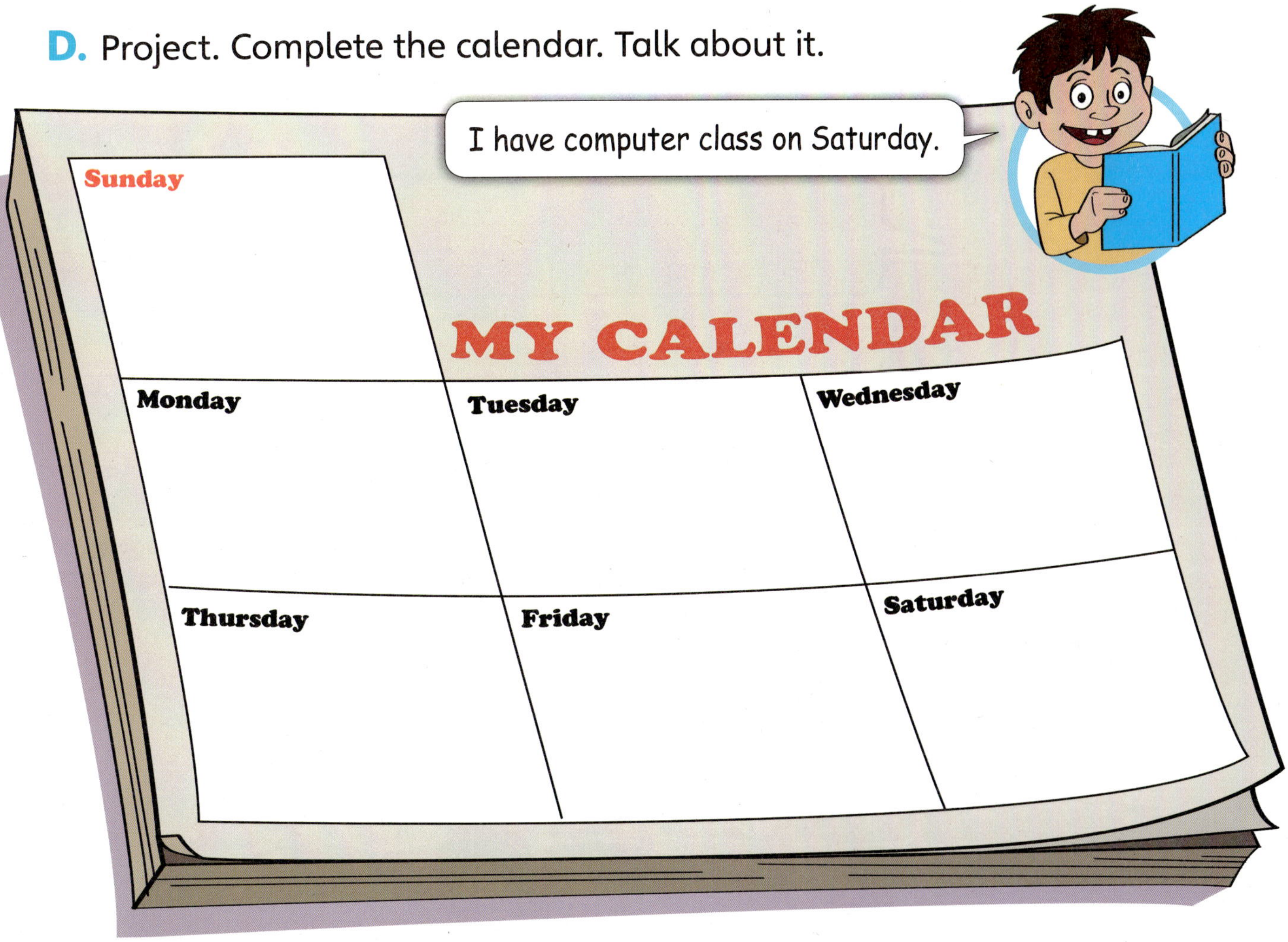

Unit 4

Daily Activities

Words

A. Track 43 Listen and point. **B.** Track 44 Listen and say.

C. Point and say.

1.  get dressed
2.  play with friends
3.  do chores
4.  have a snack
5.  brush my teeth
6.  take a shower

D. Remember. Act it out and guess.

Patterns

A. Track 45 Listen and say.

in the morning	
in the afternoon	
in the evening	

B. Read the sentences. Write the words.

1

You ________ play with friends in the evening.

2

You ________ take a shower in the afternoon.

3

We ________ have a snack in the evening.

4

They ________ do chores in the morning.

C. Practice with a partner. Talk about yourselves.

Words

A. Track 46 Listen and point. **B.** Track 47 Listen and say. **C.** Point and say.

1 
eat breakfast

2 
go to school

3 
go home

4 
do homework

5 
have dinner

6 
go to bed

D. Circle and write.

1 

have
do ______

2 

go to
do ______

3 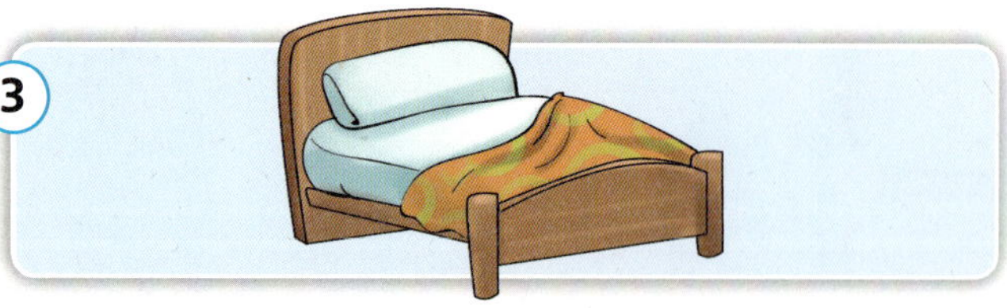

go to
have ______

4 

eat
go ______

E. Remember. Talk about yourselves.

Patterns

A. Track 48 Listen and say.

B. Read the sentences. Write the words.

1 ________ you eat breakfast at 9:00?

No, we don't.

2 Do ________ go home at 3:30?

Yes, they do.

3 Do they have dinner at 7:45?

________, they don't.

4 Do you do your homework at 4:00?

No, I ________.

C. Practice with a partner. Talk about yourselves.

D. Track 49 Sing the song. Go to page 77.

Conversation

A. Track 50 Listen and point. **B.** Track 51 Listen and say.

C. Track 52 Listen. Then practice with the new words.

steak iced tea

D. Role-play the dialogue.

E. **Value** Write a check (✓) or an (✗).

A. Track 53 Listen and say.

Long e

tea

green

Short e

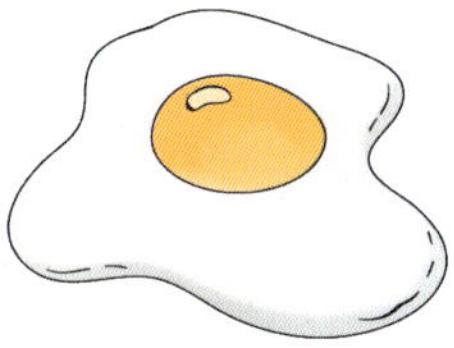
egg

pen

B. Track 54 Listen and check (✓).

1

2

3
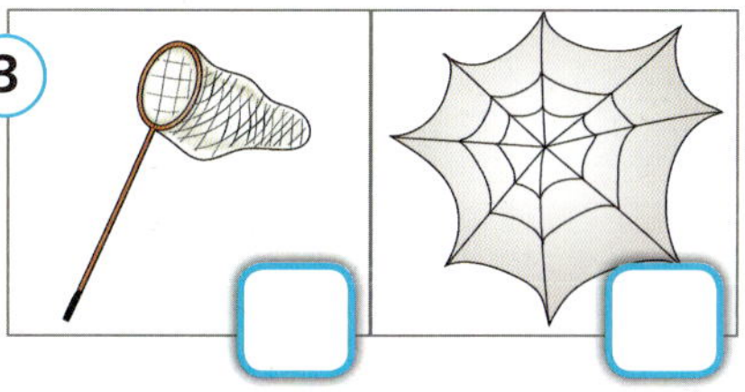

4

5

6

C. Track 55 Listen and match.

1	2	3	4	5
men	seal	seam	mean	sell

D. Read the words.

1. feed
lead
weed

2. fed
led
wed

3. beet
meet
seat

4. bet
met
set

Reading 2

Ellie Peters and Her Family

A. Track 56 Listen and follow along.

1 Ellie Peters and her family live on a farm. They all get up at 5:30 in the morning.

2 The girls get eggs. Mark and Mr. Peters milk the cows.

3 They eat breakfast at 7:00. They have eggs, bread, fruit and milk. It's a healthy breakfast.

4 The children go to school at 8:00. They go to the same school. They go by bus. The school is small.

D. Read and write *Yes* or *No*.

________ **1.** The Peters get up at 5:30.

________ **2.** Ellie and Sarah milk the cows.

B. Track 57 Listen, read and say.

C. Read with a partner.

5

The children go home at 3:30. Ellie and Sarah ride their horses. Mark and Mr. Peters fix the barn.

6

After dinner, the family goes to the living room. Ellie and Sarah play a game. Mark uses the computer. Mr. and Mrs. Peters watch TV.

7

Ellie goes to bed at 8:30. She and her father read a storybook. Good night, Ellie.

New Words • same • fix • after • use

_______ **3.** The children go home at 3:00.

_______ **4.** The Peters go to bed at 8:30.

Review 1

A. Complete the puzzle. Then write and draw.

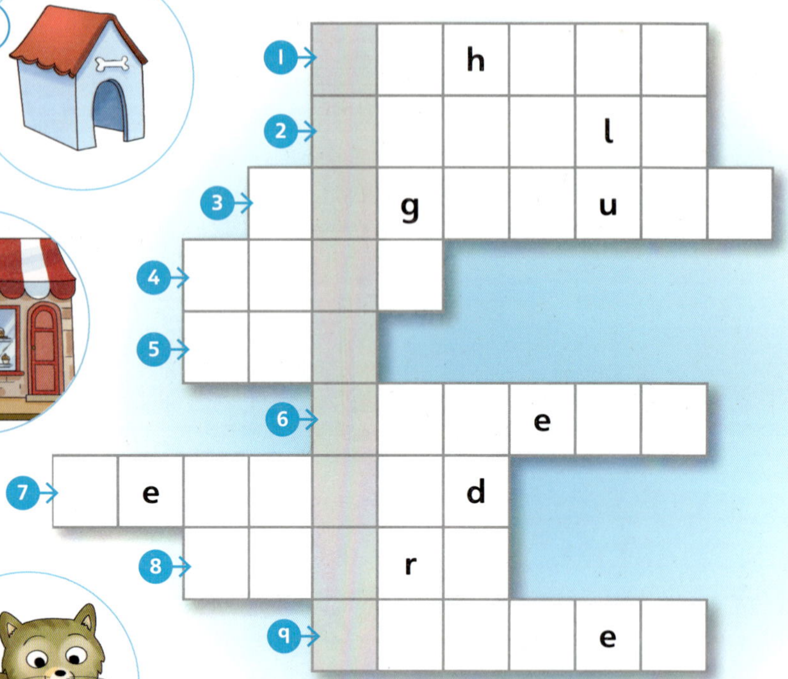

What does he have?

He has a ______________.

B. Track 58 Listen and check (✓).

C. Read and match.

1	brush	with friends
2	play	a snack
3	take	homework
4	do	to bed
5	go	my teeth
6	have	a shower

a

b

c

d

e

f

D. Track 59 Listen and check (✓) *Yes* or *No*.

1

Yes
No

2

Yes
No

3

Yes
No

4

Yes
No

5

Yes
No

6

Yes
No

Review 1

E. Write *have*, *has*, *don't have* or *doesn't have*.

1 

I ____________ music class on Monday.

2 

He ____________ a hamster cage.

3 

She ____________ kung fu class on Friday.

4 

He ____________ a goldfish bowl.

5 

They ____________ a puppy.

F. Track 60 Listen and circle.

1. a. What does he have?
   b. Does he have a kitten?
2. a. Is she going home?
   b. Where's she going?
3. a. Do they do chores in the morning?
   b. Do you do chores in the morning?
4. a. Do you have English class on Thursday?
   b. Does he have English class on Thursday?

G. Track 61 Listen and write a, b, c or d.

1

2

3

4

H. Say the word and circle.

1

long a short a

2

long a short a

3

long a short a

4

long a short a

5

long e short e

6

long e short e

7

long e short e

8

long e short e

Unit 5

Things We Wear

Words

A. Track 62 Listen and point. **B.** Track 63 Listen and say.

C. Point and say.

1.  jacket
2.  shirt
3.  pants
4.  shorts
5.  jeans
6.  sneakers

D. Remember. Talk about yourselves.

Patterns

A. Track 64 Listen and say.

I – my
you – your
he – his
she – her
they – their
we – our

B. Read the sentences. Write the words.

1

These are ________ shorts.

2

This is ________ shirt.

3

These are ________ sneakers.

4

These are ________ pants.

C. Practice with a partner. Use your own things.

Words

A. Track 65 Listen and point. **B.** Track 66 Listen and say. **C.** Point and say.

1

wet

2

dry

3
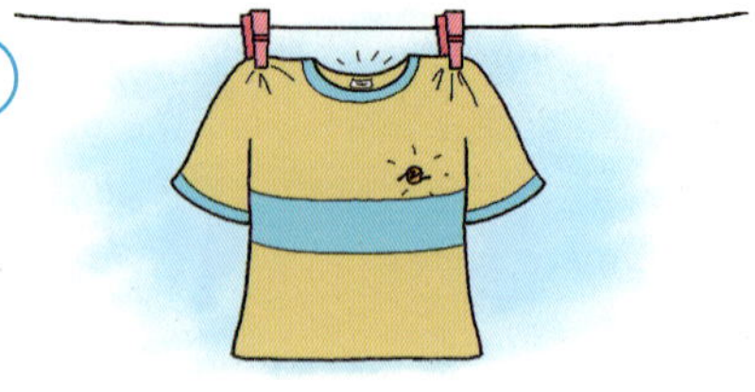
clean

4

dirty

5

tight

6

loose

D. Match and write.

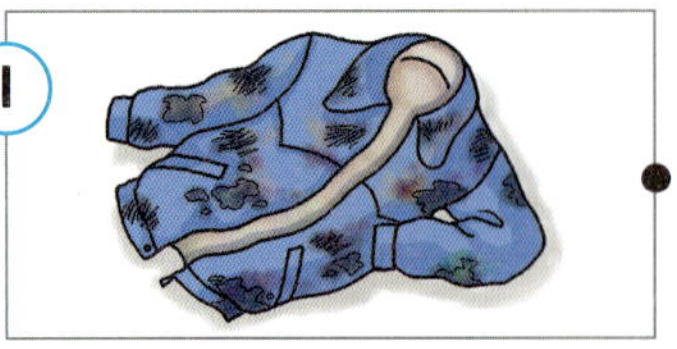

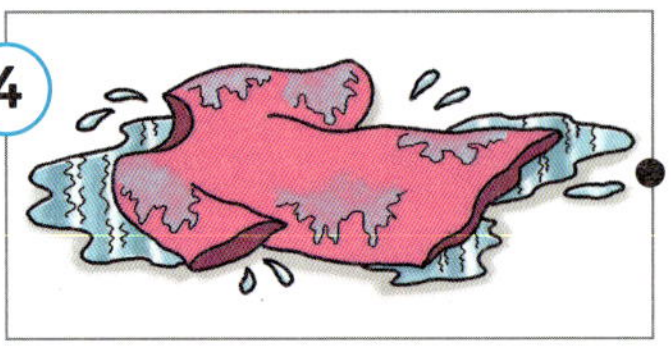

- a. The sneakers are ______________.
- b. The shirt is ______________.
- c. The jacket is ______________.
- d. The jeans are ______________.

E. Remember. Talk about yourselves.

Patterns

A. Track 67 Listen and say.

B. Read the sentences. Write the words.

1

These ________ are ________.

These are ________ ________.

2

That ________ is ________.

That is a ________ ________.

3

These ________ are ________.

These are ________ ________.

4

Those ________ are ________.

Those are ________ ________.

C. Practice with a partner. Talk about yourselves.

D. Track 68 Sing the song. Go to page 78.

Conversation

A. Track 69 Listen and point. **B.** Track 70 Listen and say.

C. Track 71 Listen. Then practice with the new words.

dirty wash

D. Role-play the dialogue.

E. **Value** Write a check (✓) or an (✗).

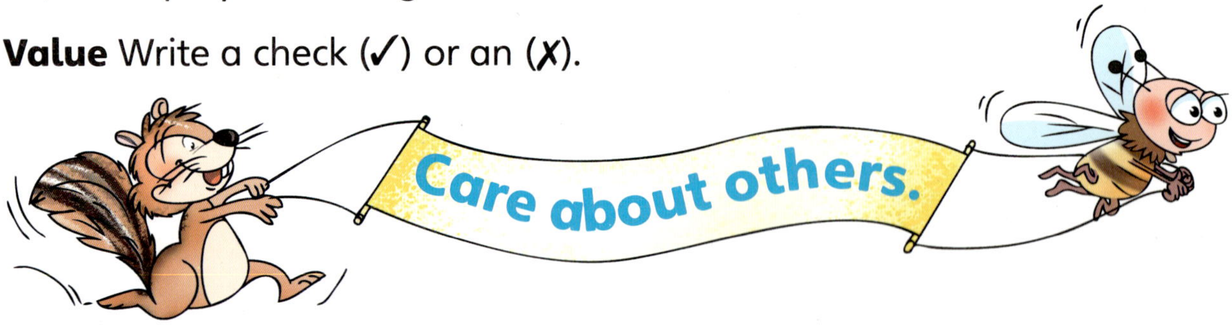

1

2

3

Sounds

A. Track 72 Listen and say.

Long i

r**i**c**e**

l**i**m**e**

n**igh**t

B. Track 73 Listen for the *long i* sound. Circle *Yes* or *No*.

1 
Yes No

2 
Yes No

3 
Yes No

4 
Yes No

5 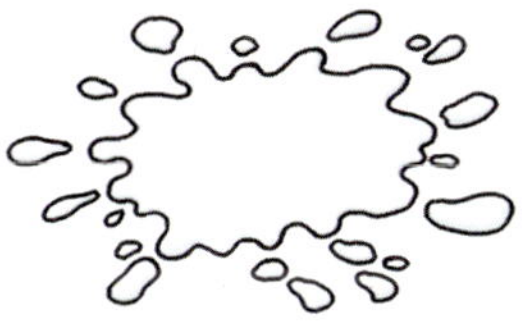
Yes No

6 
Yes No

C. Track 74 Listen and check (✓).

1. ☐ might ☐ night
2. ☐ fine ☐ vine
3. ☐ ride ☐ ripe
4. ☐ lime ☐ mile

D. Read the words.

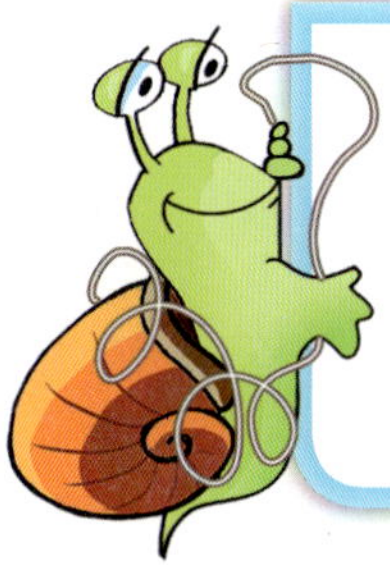

1. hide, ride, wide
2. dime, lime, time
3. fire, hire, wire
4. right, sight, tight

Expansion 3

A. Write an X on the one that doesn't belong.

1	shorts	jacket	shirt
2	jeans	shirt	pants
3	sneakers	jeans	shorts
4	jeans	pants	shorts
5	shorts	sneakers	pants

B. Look, read and match. Then match to the opposites.

1 	wet	dirty	a 
2 	clean	loose	b 
3 	tight	dry	c 

C. What about you? Read, check (✓) and write.

1. I like my
   - ☐ jeans.
   - ☐ pants.
   - ☐ sneakers.
   - ☐ shirt.
   - ☐ jacket.
   - ☐ shorts.

2. My shirt is
   - ☐ dry.
   - ☐ clean.
   - ☐ loose.
   - ☐ dirty.
   - ☐ tight.
   - ☐ wet.

3. My sneakers are ____________ and ____________ .

D. Project. Draw your favorite clothes. Talk about them.

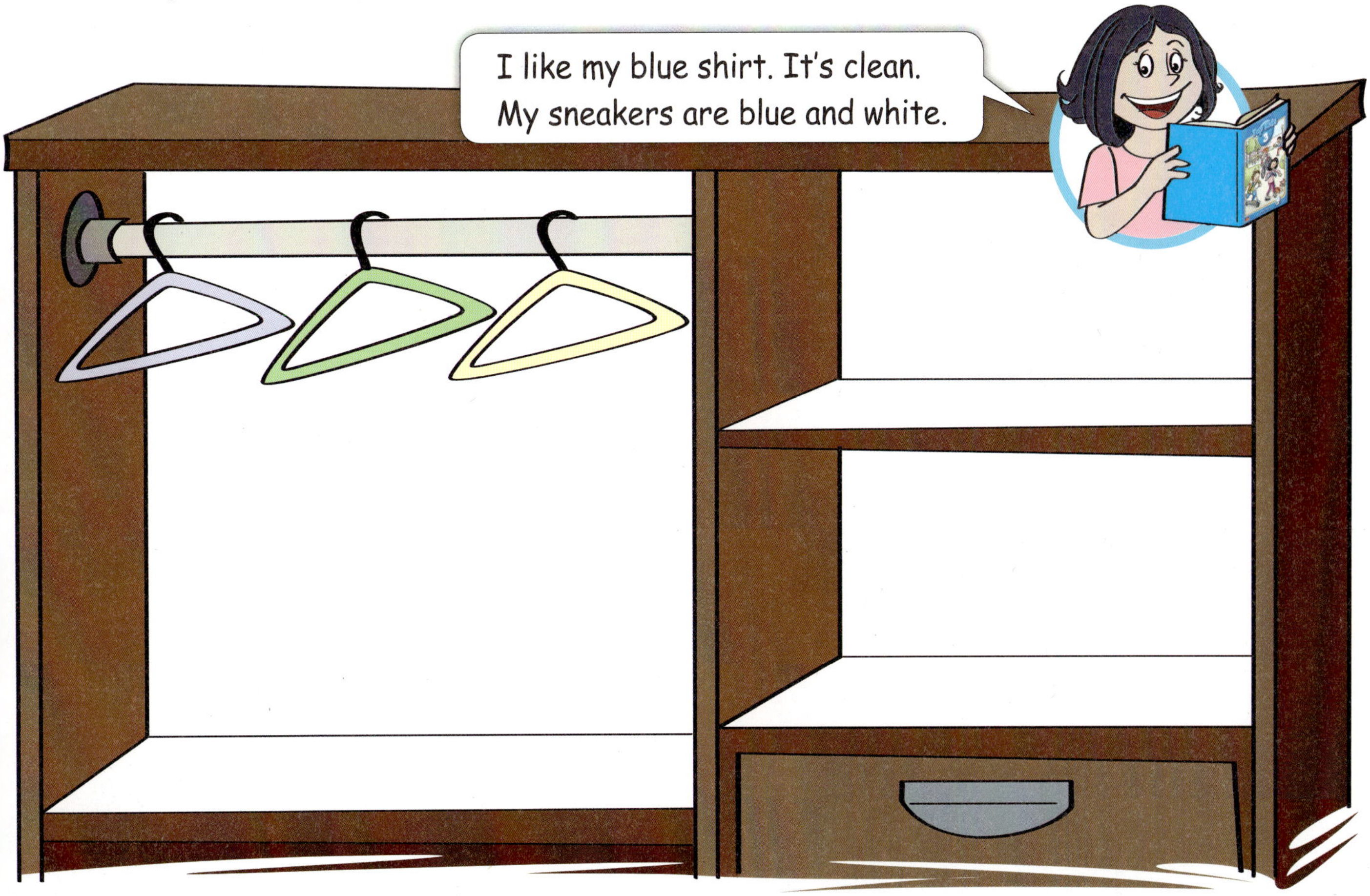

Unit 6

My Room

Words

A. Track 75 Listen and point.

B. Track 76 Listen and say.

C. Point and say.

1.  alarm clock
2. 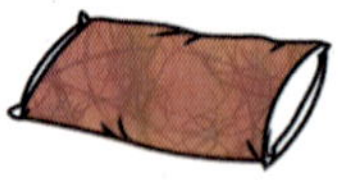 pillow
3. 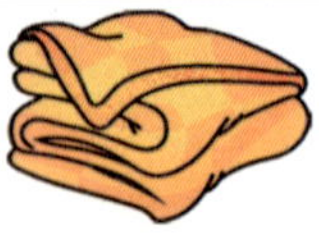 blanket
4.  dresser
5.  lamp
6.  rug

D. Remember. Talk about yourselves.

Patterns

A. Track 77 Listen and say.

B. Read the sentences. Write the words.

1 The keys are ________ the rug.

2 The pillow is ________ the bed.

3 The blanket is ________ ________ ________ the door.

4 The baseballs are ________ the dresser.

C. Practice with a partner. Talk about the classroom.

Words

A. Track 78 Listen and point. **B.** Track 79 Listen and say. **C.** Point and say.

1 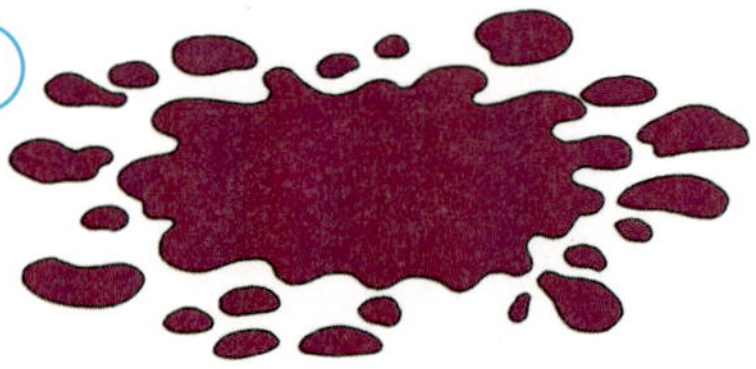
purple

2 
orange

3 
brown

4 
pink

5 
gold

6 
silver

D. Match and write.

1 

2 

3 

4 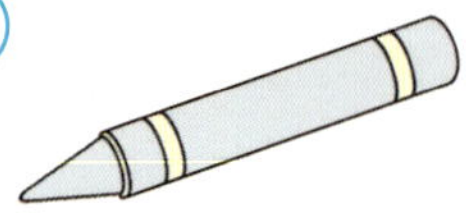

a. 

It's ______________.

b. 
It's ______________.

c. 
It's ______________.

d. 
It's ______________.

E. Remember. Talk about yourselves.

Patterns

A. Track 80 Listen and say.

B. Read the sentences. Write the words.

1

______ are the crayons?

They're ______ ______ the tablet.

2

______ is the blanket?

It's ______ the pillows.

3

Where ______ the jacket?

It's ______ the shirts.

4

Where ______ the pillows?

They're ______ ______ the dresser.

C. Practice with a partner. Talk about yourselves.

D. Track 81 Sing the song. Go to page 78.

Conversation

A. Track 82 Listen and point.

B. Track 83 Listen and say.

C. Track 84 Listen. Then practice with the new words.

Put away　　later

D. Role-play the dialogue.

E. **Value** Write a check (✓) or an (✗).

1 

2 

3 

Sounds

A. Track 85 Listen and say.

Long i

bike

kite

Short i

6
six

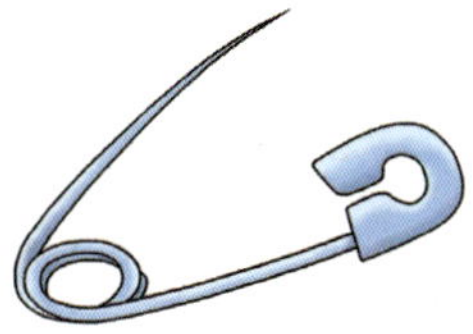
pin

B. Track 86 Listen and match.

1 

2 

3 

long i

short i

4 

5 

6 

C. Track 87 Listen and number.

☐ hide ☐ light ☐ dim ☐ hid ☐ lit ☐ dime

D. Read the words.

1.	2.	3.	4.
file	fill	bite	bit
mile	mill	kite	kit
pile	pill	site	sit

Reading 3

Brothers

A. Track 88 Listen and follow along.

This is Ben and Tim's bedroom. It has two beds, a dresser and a desk.

Tim is noisy.
He talks, shouts and sings.
He plays with Ben's toys and hamster. Ben isn't happy.

Ben's family moves to a big house. Ben has a bedroom. Tim has a bedroom, too. Ben's room is quiet and neat. Ben is very happy.

D. Read and write *Yes* or *No*.

_______ **1.** Ben and Tim are brothers.

_______ **2.** Ben's family moves to a small house.

B. Track 89 Listen, read and say.

C. Read with a partner.

Ben reads a book.
He does his homework.
He plays with the hamster.
But Ben is lonely.

There's a knock on the door.
Tim comes in.
Ben hugs Tim.
Tim hugs Ben.
They're happy to be together.

Tim talks, shouts and sings.
He plays with Ben's toys and hamster.
But Ben isn't angry.
He's happy.

New Words 8 • noisy • move • lonely • miss • knock • hug

_______ **3.** Ben is noisy and messy.

_______ **4.** Ben misses Tim.

Unit 7 Show and Tell

Words

A. Track 90 Listen and point. **B.** Track 91 Listen and say.

C. Point and say.

1.  panda
2.  elephant
3.  giraffe
4.  kangaroo
5.  shark
6.  penguin

D. Remember. Talk about yourselves.

Patterns

A. Track 92 Listen and say.

I – mine
you – yours
he – his
she – hers

B. Read the sentences. Write the words.

1

________ elephant is this?

It's ________.

2

________ panda is this?

It's ________.

3

________ giraffe is this?

It's ________.

4

________ kangaroo is this?

It's ________.

C. Practice with a partner. Talk about classmates' things.

Words

A. Track 93 Listen and point. **B.** Track 94 Listen and say. **C.** Point and say.

1

nervous

2

bored

3

excited

4

scared

5

worried

6

proud

D. Look and write.

1

He's ______________.

2

She's ______________.

3

They're ______________.

4

I'm ______________.

E. Remember. Talk about yourselves.

Patterns

A. Track 95 Listen and say.

B. Read the sentences. Write the words.

1 

Look at ________. He's bored.

2 

Look at ________. She's scared.

3 

Look at ________. I'm worried.

4 

Look at ________. She's excited.

C. Practice with a partner. Use your books.

D. Track 96 Sing the song. Go to page 79.

Conversation

A. Track 97 Listen and point.

B. Track 98 Listen and say.

C. Track 99 Listen. Then practice with the new words.

great   wrong

D. Role-play the dialogue.

E. **Value** Write a check (✓) or an (✗).

1

2

3

A. Track 100 Listen and say.

Long o

goat

road

home

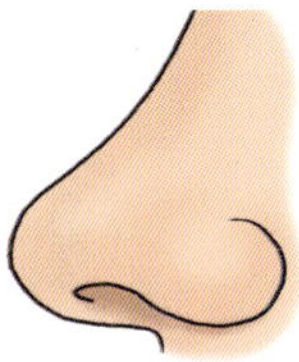
nose

B. Track 101 Listen. Write a check (✓) if the word has a *long o* sound.

1 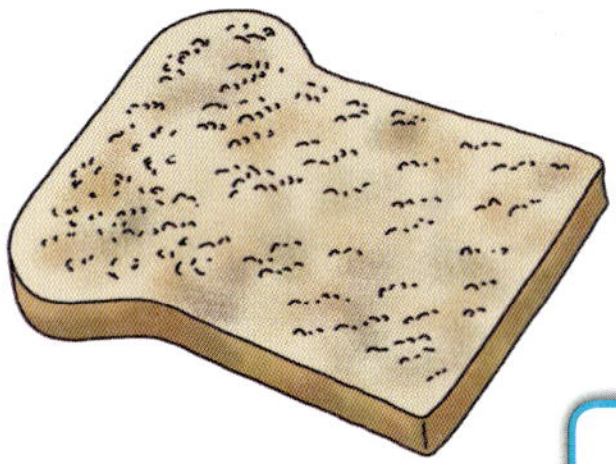 ☐

2 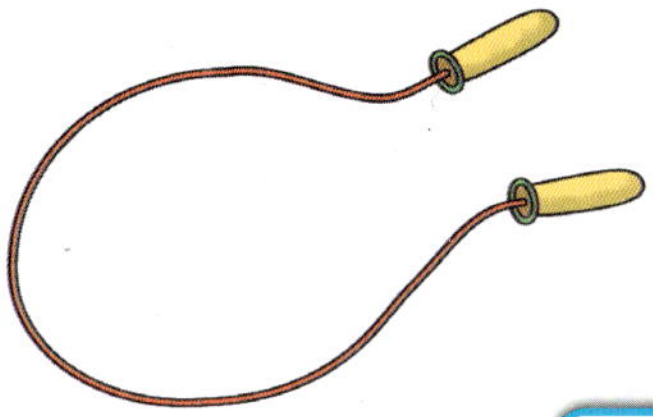 ☐

3  ☐

4 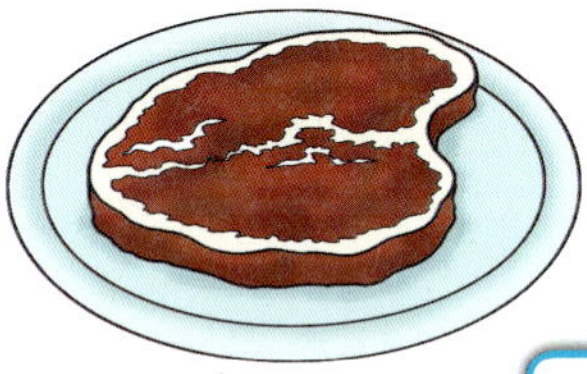 ☐

5  ☐

6  ☐

C. Track 102 Listen and match.

1 2 3 4 5

rope oak note soap moan

D. Read the words.

1.	2.	3.	4.
boat	coast	bone	hose
coat	roast	cone	pose
goat	toast	tone	rose

Expansion 4

A. Look, read and write.

1

It can't swim.

It's a ______________.

2

It isn't black and white.

It's a ______________.

3

It can't run.

It's a ______________.

4

It's small.

It's a ______________.

5

It doesn't eat fish.

It's an ______________.

B. Look and circle.

1

She's bored. / nervous.

2

He's excited. / scared.

3

He's scared. / proud.

4

She's worried. / proud.

C. What about you? Read, check (✓) and write.

1. I can make a/an
   - panda.
   - elephant.
   - giraffe.
   - kangaroo.
   - shark.
   - penguin.

2. I like

   - giraffes.
   - penguins.
   - elephants.
   - sharks.
   - pandas.
   - kangaroos.

3. I am …
   - bored
   - happy
   - excited
   - nervous
   - worried
   - proud

   today.

D. Project. Draw your favorite animal. Talk about it.

Unit

8

At the Supermarket

Words

A. Track 103 Listen and point.

B. Track 104 Listen and say.

C. Point and say.

1.  cheese
2.  peanut butter
3. 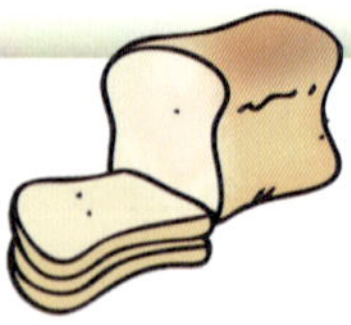 bread
4.  cucumber
5.  potato
6.  pear

D. Remember. Use your books. Point and say.

Patterns

A. Track 105 Listen and say.

B. Read the sentences. Write the words.

1

You ________ ________ potatoes.

2

I ________ ________ peanut butter.

3

They ________ ________ bread.

4

You ________ ________ cucumbers.

C. Practice with a partner. Talk about yourselves.

A. Track 106 Listen and point. **B.** Track 107 Listen and say. **C.** Point and say.

1

potato chips

2

nuts

3

crackers

4

popcorn

5

pudding

6
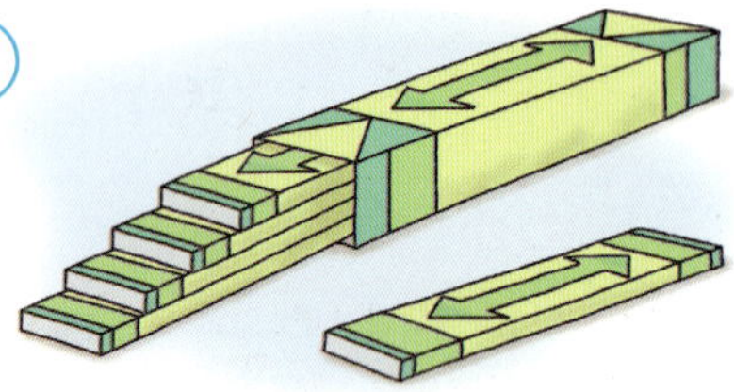
gum

D. Look and write.

1

She likes ______________________.

2

He likes ______________________.

3

I like ______________________.

4

They like ______________________.

E. Remember. Talk about yourselves.

Patterns

A. Track 108 Listen and say.

B. Read the sentences. Write the words.

1

You _______ _______ _______ pudding.

2

We _______ _______ _______ gum.

3

You _______ _______ _______ potato chips.

4

I _______ _______ _______ nuts.

C. Practice with a partner. Talk about yourselves.

D. Track 109 Sing the song. Go to page 79.

Conversation

A. Track 110 Listen and point.

B. Track 111 Listen and say.

C. Track 112 Listen. Then practice with the new words.

Pardon　　nuts

D. Role-play the dialogue.

E. **Value** Write a check (✓) or an (✗).

1

2

3

A. Track 113 Listen and say.

Long O

coat

note

Short O

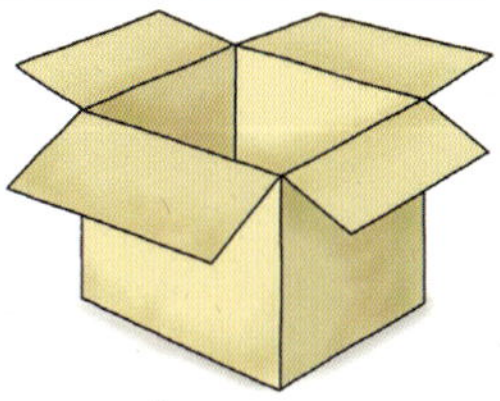

box

pot

B. Track 114 Listen and circle.

1 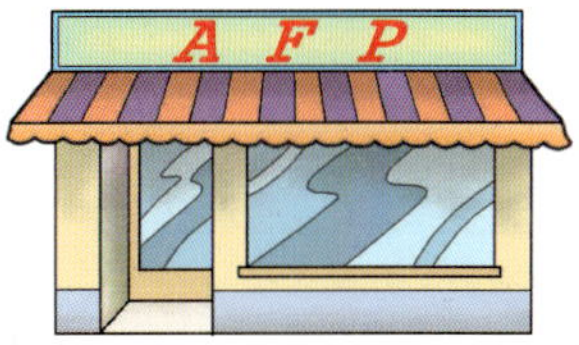

long o short o

2 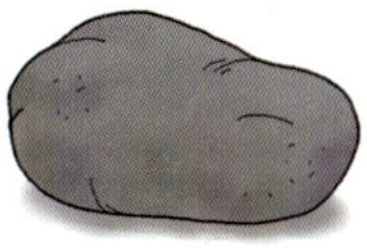

long o short o

3 

long o short o

4 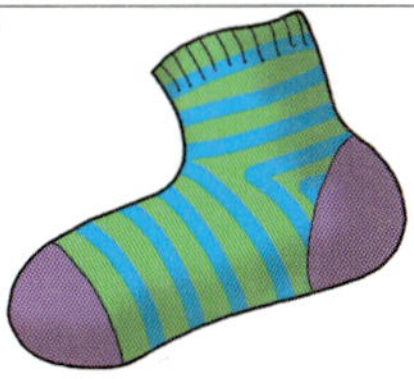

long o short o

5 

long o short o

6 

long o short o

C. Track 115 Listen and check (✓).

1. ☐ goat ☐ got
2. ☐ joke ☐ jock
3. ☐ soap ☐ sop
4. ☐ note ☐ not

D. Read the words.

1. code	2. cod	3. hope	4. hop
mode	mod	mope	mop
rode	rod	pope	pop

Reading 4

Amy and Sam's Habits

A. Track 116 Listen and follow along.

1 This is Amy. She has healthy habits. She eats good food. She likes nuts and pears.

2 This is Sam. He doesn't have healthy habits. He likes pudding and popcorn.

3 Amy gets up at 6:30. She eats a healthy breakfast. She runs to school. She's never late.

4 Sam gets up at 7:30. He doesn't eat breakfast. He walks to school. He's always late.

D. Read and write *Yes* or *No*.

______ **1.** Sam has healthy habits.

______ **2.** Amy runs to school.

B. Track 117 Listen, read and say.

5

Amy likes exercise. After school, Amy goes to the park. She and her friends ride their bikes.

7

After dinner, Amy does homework. She takes a shower and brushes her teeth. She goes to bed at 8:30.

C. Read with a partner.

6

Sam doesn't like exercise. He watches TV after school. He plays computer games, too.

8

Sam watches TV after dinner. He takes a shower, but he doesn't brush his teeth. He goes to bed at 11:00.

Who are you like, Amy or Sam?

New Words 8 • habit • never • late • always • exercise

_______ **3.** Sam likes exercise.

_______ **4.** Amy watches TV at night.

Review 2

A. Look and complete the puzzles.

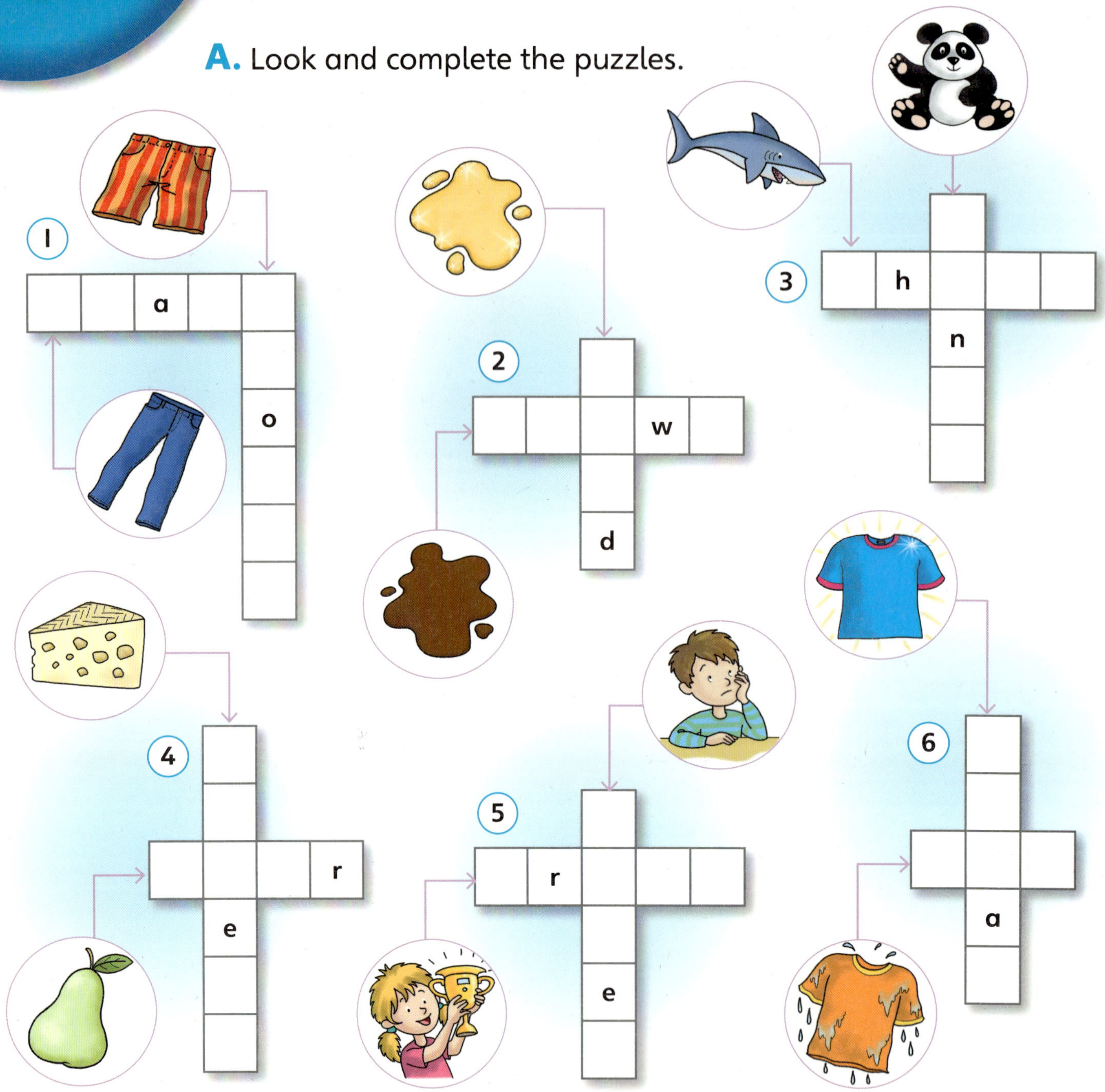

B. Track 118 Listen and number.

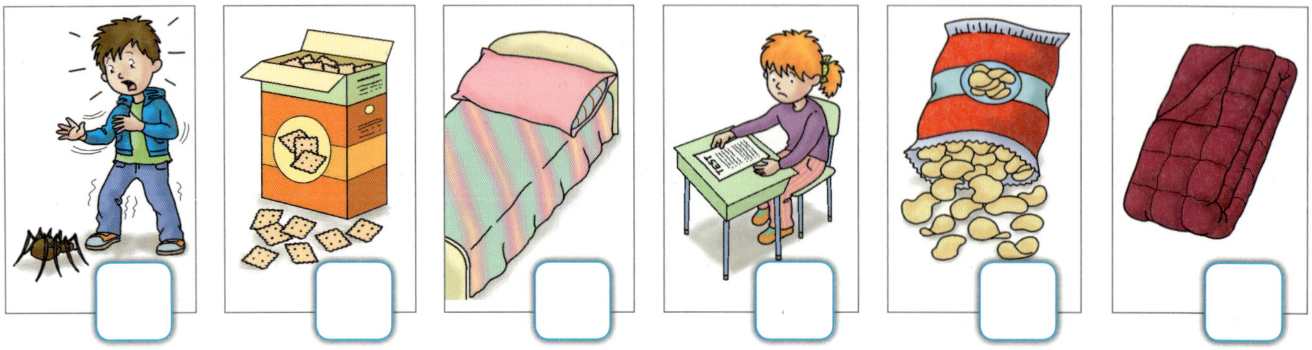

C. Look and write.

excited	orange	tight	dirty	silver
lamps	sneakers	penguins	shirt	dresser

1 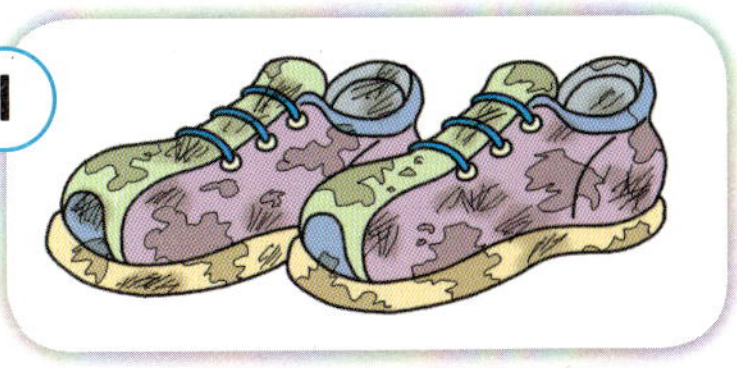

They're ________ ________.

2 

It's an ________ ________.

3 

They're ________ ________.

4 

It's a ________ ________.

5 

They're ________ ________.

D. Track Listen and check (✓) *Yes* or *No*.

1 

☐ Yes
☐ No

2 

☐ Yes
☐ No

3 

☐ Yes
☐ No

4 

☐ Yes
☐ No

5 

☐ Yes
☐ No

6 

☐ Yes
☐ No

Review 2

E. Look and write the correct words.

1 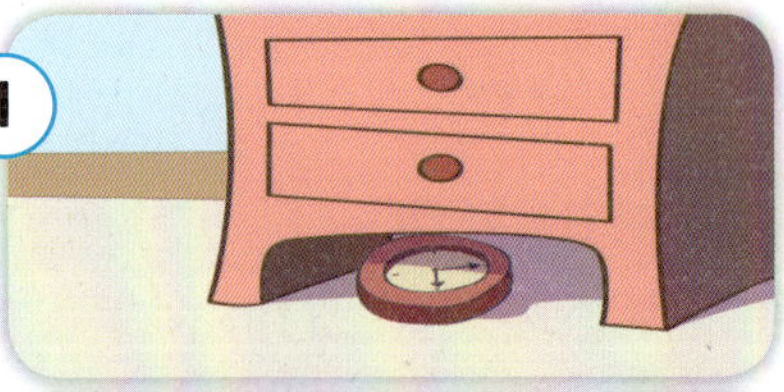

________ the pink alarm clock? (Where's/Whose)

It's ________ the dresser. (in front of/under)

2 

Look at ________. (he/him)

________ nervous. (He's /His)

3 

________ kangaroo is this? (Where/Whose)

It's ________. (mine/me)

4 

They don't want ________ bread. (some/any)

They want ________ potatoes. (some/any)

5 

Look at ________. (her/she)

The penguin is ________. (her/hers)

F. Unscramble the sentences.

1. any / They / peanut butter. / want / don't

   ____

2. shirt. / a / This / is / loose

   ____

3. want / I / pudding. / some

   ____

4. is / dry. / jacket / This

   ____

5. between / The blanket / the pillows. / is

   ____

G. Track 120 Listen and write *a*, *b*, *c* or *d*.

1

2

3

4

H. Say the word and circle.

1

long i short i

2

long i short i

3

long i short i

4

long i short i

5

long o short o

6

long o short o

7

long o short o

8

long o short o

Songs

Unit 1: Page 7

Hey! Where's He Going?

(To the tune of *The Farmer in the Dell*)

He has a baseball.
He has a baseball.
Hey! Where's he going?
He's going to the park.

She has a key.
She has a key.
Hey! Where's she going?
She's going home.

He has a storybook.
He has a storybook.
Hey! Where's he going?
He's going to the library.

Unit 2: Page 15

What Does She Have?

(To the tune of *Good Night Ladies*)

What does she have?
What does she have?
What does she have?
She has a goldfish bowl.
She has a new goldfish bowl, goldfish bowl, goldfish bowl.
She has a new goldfish bowl, and a nice big goldfish.

What does he have?
What does he have?
What does he have?
He has a hamster cage.
He has a new hamster cage, hamster cage, hamster cage.
He has a new hamster cage, and a nice big hamster.

Unit 3: Page 23

On Monday

(To the tune of *London Bridge*)

She has ballet class on Monday.
On Monday.
On Monday.
She has ballet class on Monday.
Today is Monday.

She has math class on Tuesday.
On Tuesday.
On Tuesday.
She has math class on Tuesday.
Tomorrow is Tuesday.

Unit 4: Page 31

Do You Go to School at 8:00?

(To the tune of *Here We Go Round the Mulberry Bush*)

Do you eat breakfast at 7:00, at 7:00, at 7:00?
Do you eat breakfast at 7:00?
Yes, I do. Do you?
Yes!

Do you do homework at 6:45, at 6:45, at 6:45?
Do you do homework at 6:45?
No, I don't. Do you?
No!

Unit 5: Page 43

Tight Jeans

(To the tune of *Are You Sleeping*?)

These are tight jeans.
These are tight jeans.
Very tight jeans.
Very tight jeans.
These jeans are very tight.
These jeans are very tight.
Very tight jeans.
Very tight jeans.

This is a clean shirt.
This is a clean shirt.
A very clean shirt.
A very clean shirt.
This shirt is very clean.
This shirt is very clean.
A very clean shirt.
A very clean shirt.

Unit 6: Page 51

Where's the Blanket?

(To the tune of *Alouette*)

Where's the blanket?
Where's the purple blanket?
Where's the blanket?
It's behind the bed.

Where's the dresser?
Where's the brown dresser?
Where's the dresser?
It's next to the bed.

Purple blanket. Brown dresser.
Purple blanket. Brown dresser.
Oh, oh, oh, oh...

Where are the pillows?
Where are the red pillows?
Where are the pillows?
They're between the lamps.

Unit 7: Page 59

I'm Excited!

(To the tune of *If You're Happy and You Know It*)

Look at me. I'm excited. Yes, I am!
Look at me. I'm excited. Yes, I am!
Look at me. I'm excited.
Look at me. I'm excited.
Look at me. I'm excited. Yes, I am!

Look at her. She's nervous. Yes, she is!
Look at her. She's nervous. Yes, she is!
Look at her. She's nervous.
Look at her. She's nervous.
Look at her. She's nervous. Yes, she is!

Look at him. He's bored. Yes, he is!
Look at him. He's bored. Yes, he is!
Look at him. He's bored.
Look at him. He's bored.
Look at him. He's bored. Yes, he is!

Unit 8: Page 67

I Don't Want Any Nuts!

(To the tune of *Head, Shoulders, Knees and Toes*)

I don't want any nuts, any nuts.
I don't want any nuts, any nuts.
No nuts for me, no nuts for me.
I don't want any nuts, any nuts.

They don't want any gum, any gum.
They don't want any gum, any gum.
No gum for them, no gum for them.
They don't want any gum, any gum.

Syllabus

	Words/Patterns 1	Words/Patterns 2	Conversation	Sounds
Unit 1 **In the Neighborhood**	**Words:** park, library, bakery, store, school, house **Patterns:** • Where's he going? • He's going to the park.	**Words:** baseball, storybook, apple pie, egg, workbook, key **Patterns:** • He has a baseball. **Song:** *Hey! Where's He Going?*	**Asking for Personal Information:** A: Where do you live? B: I live in Baytown. A: Really? Me, too. B: It's a friendly place. **Value:** Be friendly.	**Long a** • a_e: cake • ai: paint • ay: gray
Expansion 1: Critical thinking, personalization, and simple project activities				
Unit 2 **Pets**	**Words:** kitten, puppy, goldfish, hamster, turtle, parrot **Patterns:** • She doesn't have a puppy.	**Words:** dog bed, cat toy, goldfish bowl, dog house, pet food, hamster cage **Patterns:** • What does she have? • She has a dog bed. **Song:** *What Does She Have?*	**Offering Help:** A: Ugh! This is heavy. B: Let me help you. A: Thanks a lot. B: No problem. **Value:** Be helpful.	**Long a and Short a** • Long a: cage, play, rain • Short a: bag, cat, pan
Reading 1: Fiction – Herby Gets a Pet				
Unit 3 **After School**	**Words:** Monday, Tuesday, Wednesday, Thursday, Friday, Saturday, Sunday **Grammar Vocab:** today, tomorrow, the day after tomorrow **Patterns:** • What day is today? • It's Monday.	**Words:** English class, math class, computer class, music class, kung fu class, ballet class **Patterns:** • I have English class on Friday. • He has music class on Saturday. **Song:** *On Monday*	**Inviting and Refusing an Invitation:** A: Can you come over today? B: No, I can't. I have to practice. A: Practice what? B: Kung fu. I have kung fu class on Friday. **Value:** Work hard.	**Long e** • ee: bee, jeep • ea: eat, leaf
Expansion 2: Critical thinking, personalization, and simple project activities				
Unit 4 **Daily Activities**	**Words:** get dressed, play with friends, do chores, have a snack, brush my teeth, take a shower **Grammar Vocab:** in the morning, in the afternoon, in the evening **Patterns:** • I don't get dressed in the evening.	**Words:** eat breakfast, go to school, go home, do homework, have dinner, go to bed **Patterns:** • Do you go to bed at 9:30? • Yes, I do. • No, they don't. **Song:** *Do You Go to School at 8:00?*	**Offering Help:** A: What's for dinner? B: Chicken and salad. A: Yum! Can I help? B: Yes. Bring me the milk, please. **Value:** Help at home.	**Long e and Short e** • Long e: tea, green • Short e: egg, pen
Reading 2: Non Fiction – Ellie Peters and Her Family				

Review 1 (Units 1-4)

	Words/Patterns 1	Words/Patterns 2	Conversation	Sounds
Unit 5 Things We Wear	**Words:** jacket, shirt, pants, shorts, jeans, sneakers **Grammar Vocab:** • I – my, you – your • he – his, she – her • they – their, we – our **Patterns:** • This is my jacket. • These are my shorts.	**Words:** wet, dry, clean, dirty, tight, loose **Patterns:** • This jacket is dry. • This is a dry jacket. • These sneakers are wet. • These are wet sneakers. **Song:** *Tight Jeans*	**Showing Sympathy/ Concern:** A: Oh, no! B: What's wrong? A: Look! My jeans are ripped. B: Don't worry. Your mom can fix them. **Value:** Care about others.	**Long i** • i_e: rice, lime • igh: night
Expansion 3: Critical thinking, personalization and simple project activities				
Unit 6 My Room	**Words:** alarm clock, pillow, blanket, dresser, lamp, rug **Grammar Vocab:** under, in front of **Patterns:** • The alarm clock is behind the lamp.	**Words:** purple, orange, brown, pink, gold, silver **Patterns:** • Where's the alarm clock? • It's next to the goldfish bowl. **Song:** *Where's the Blanket?*	**Giving Orders:** A: Your room is messy! B: Sorry. A: Pick up your toys! B: OK. I'll do it tomorrow. A: No! Please do it now! **Value:** Listen to your parents.	**Long i and Short i** • Long i: bike, kite • Short i: six, pin
Reading 3: Fiction – Brothers				
Unit 7 Show and Tell	**Words:** panda, elephant, giraffe, kangaroo, shark, penguin **Grammar Vocab:** • I – mine, you – yours • he – his, she – hers **Patterns:** • Whose shark is this? • It's mine.	**Words:** nervous, bored, excited, scared, worried, proud **Grammar Vocab:** • I – me • he – him, she – her **Patterns:** • Look at me. I'm nervous. **Song:** *I'm Excited!*	**Apologizing:** A: This is fun. B: Yes, it is. I want to go next. A: You can't. It's her turn. B: Sorry. I was rude. **Value:** Take turns.	**Long o** • oa: goat, road • o_e: home, nose
Expansion 4: Critical thinking, personalization and simple project activities				
Unit 8 At the Supermarket	**Words:** cheese, peanut butter, bread, cucumber, potato, pear **Patterns:** • I want some pears.	**Words:** potato chips, nuts, crackers, popcorn, pudding, gum **Patterns:** • I don't want any crackers. **Song:** *I Don't Want Any Nuts!*	**Buying Something:** A: Excuse me. How much is this? B: Two dollars. A: And the gum? B: One dollar. A: Here's your change. Two dollars. B: Thank you very much. **Value:** Be polite.	**Long o and Short o** • Long o: coat, note • Short o: box, pot
Reading 4: Non Fiction – Amy and Sam's Habits				

Review 2 (Units 5-8)

Word List

Unit 1

apple pie
bakery
baseball
egg
home
house
key
library
park
school
store
storybook
workbook

Unit 3

ballet class
computer class
English class
Friday
kung fu class
math class
Monday
music class
Thursday
Tuesday
Saturday
Sunday
Wednesday

Unit 5

clean
dirty
dry
jacket
jeans
loose
pants
shirt
shorts
sneakers
tight
wet

Unit 7

bored
elephant
excited
giraffe
kangaroo
nervous
panda
penguin
proud
scared
shark
worried

Unit 2

cat toy
dog bed
dog house
goldfish
goldfish bowl
hamster
hamster cage
kitten
pet food
parrot
puppy
turtle

Unit 4

brush my teeth
do chores
do homework
eat breakfast
get dressed
go to bed
go home
go to school
have a snack
have dinner
play with friends
take a shower

Unit 6

alarm clock
bed
blanket
brown
dresser
gold
lamp
orange
pillow
pink
purple
rug
silver

Unit 8

bread
cheese
crackers
cucumber
gum
nuts
peanut butter
pear
popcorn
potato
potato chips
pudding

How to Use the App

EnglishCentral

1. Scan the QR code at the back of the book.

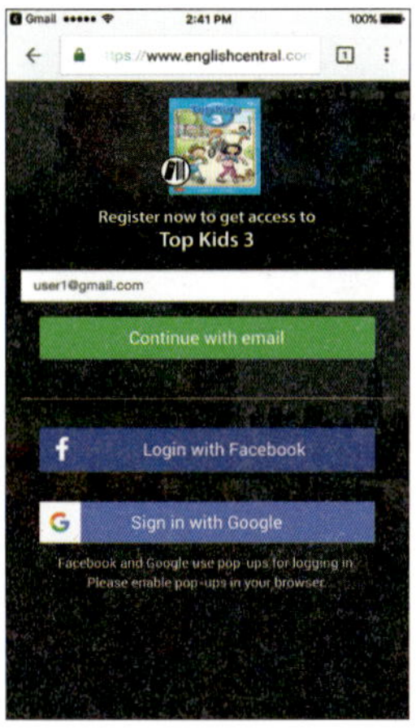

2. Type your email address. Then click on "Continue with email."

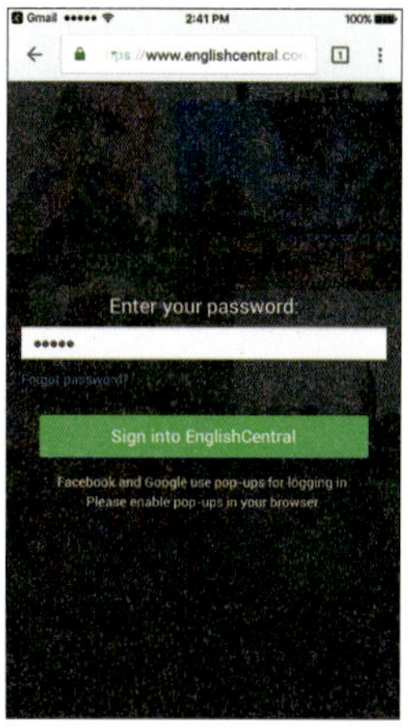

3a. If you already have an EnglishCentral account, enter your password.

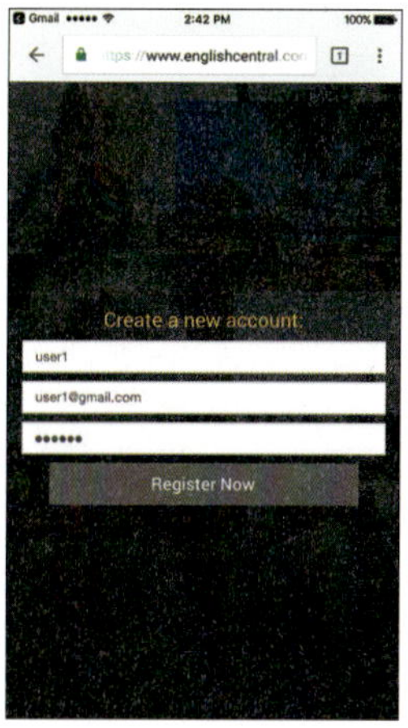

3b. If you don't have an EnglishCentral account, add your name, email, and password. Then click on "Register Now."

4. You now have the textbook course in your account. Click on "START."

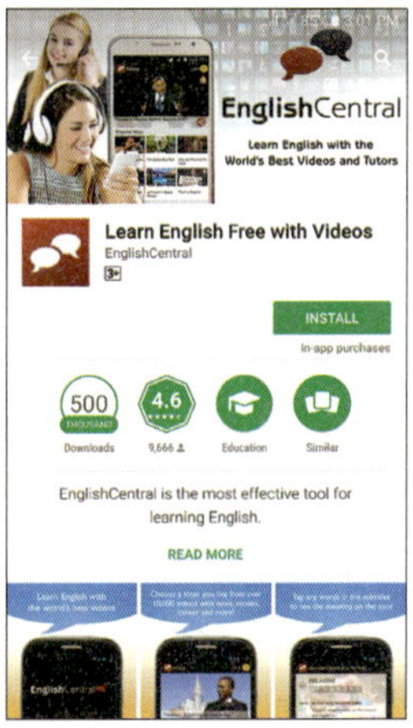

5. Install the EnglishCentral app.

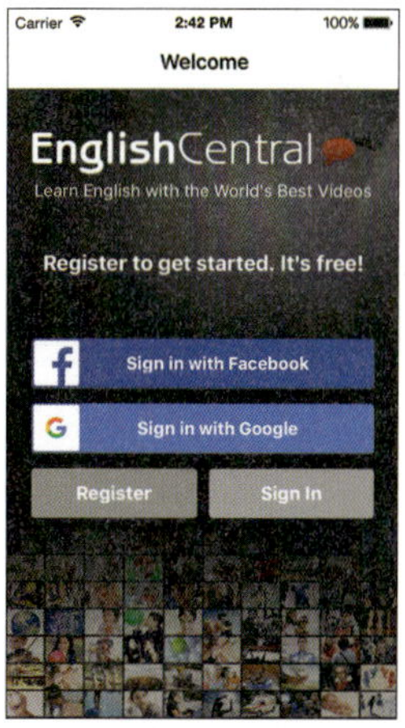

6. Click on "Sign In." Sign in with the email address that you used in #2.

7. You will see your textbook course when you log in. Complete all the units to finish the course.